DDJ PUBLISHING

HOW TO MAKE GREAT MUSIC WITHOUT FORMAL TRAINING

Keys for a Unique Sound and Style, Beginner or Pro. Perform, Arrange, and Compose with Fast, Easy Lessons. Hone Playing Skills and Artistic Creativity

"None of us could read music... None of us can write it." John Lennon admitted about the Beatles, *"but as pure musicians, as inspired humans to make the noise ... as good as anybody."*

"To play a wrong note is insignificant; to play without passion is inexcusable."
- Beethoven

"Music gives a soul to the universe, wings to the mind, flight to the imagination, and life to everything."
- Plato

Contents

1

Introduction

Have you ever wanted to pick up an instrument and just play music? Have you never had formal training, but are still drawn to the idea of being a musician? It may seem like it's too late in life, and if you didn't start at an early age, then it's probably just a hopeless dream.

From what we traditionally know, learning to play an instrument, including singing, takes hours of dedicated, daily practice, discipline, or inborn talent. You just don't want to put in countless hours of practice, besides, you couldn't read a single musical note, if you're life depended on it.

Perhaps you've even tried to take piano, guitar, or other lessons, but it just didn't work out. You learned a scale or two, perhaps played a simple nursery rhyme song. In the end it just didn't seem worth the effort to follow through.

If only there was a way to approach music with a simpler, more practical method for learning. Well, I have some good news to share with you.

There are some incredibly easy to learn ideas that can actually have you playing in no time. I mean playing the kind of music you love to listen to and have only dreamed of playing yourself.

It doesn't' require you to be highly knowledgeable of all the music theories and principles that are traditionally taught. You don't need to be greatly gifted either. A very basic and minimal amount of musical knowledge is plenty. Knowing just the basics or what little you already do know is enough for anyone. Sound great and perform for others if you choose or simply for your own satisfaction.

The learning process itself doesn't need to be so technical and complex. With the right approach, you will be amazed at what you can achieve in understanding and performing music in a relatively short amount of time. This is what you will learn in this short and concise book.

You will learn a straightforward method that gets you playing and understanding music faster. Plus you'll start learning to implement the elements of music in a better way. I'll share musical insight and basic knowledge that will serve you as the music maker and creator. My hope is that it opens up a whole new dimension in life for you.

You'll learn of valuable concepts about your music on whatever level you desire whether as musician, performer, artist, composer or even producer. This book is all about artistic musical creation, and how to make great music without formal training.

2

Musical Appeal

So what is music's significance anyway, and why is it so impactful for us? To the untrained in musical terminology and without formal education, how it works may be a big mystery. The mystery is actually part of its magic though.

Why is music so universally appealing and meaningful to so many people of all backgrounds? These are great questions and the answer has certainly been researched by musicologists, sociologists, evolutionary psychologists and others.

The bottom line is that music is full of wonder and it's a gift. Its origins go back to our earliest days as humans. There was an element of social bonding created as we struggled to survive in ancient times. We have certainly inherited remnants of those feelings and social bonds. When we become avid listeners to music today, whether it is classical, traditional folk, popular or rock music it holds a power inside us that is undeniable.

Music making is a passionate, emotional outlet, a creative skill, and a powerful artform. As such it is capable of "imitating" life and its feelings, excitement, and entire range of human experiences. We can tell stories, share thoughts, and spread our messages far and wide.

Yes, it is a gift to be appreciated. You can be a part of it and not only as a listener. You can be a creator and performer, if not for a large audience, then just for your close friends or yourself. All it really takes is some basic knowledge of how it works, good building blocks, and the cues to get you going in the right direction.

Musical Elements, Just the Basics:

As mentioned, we need to take into account just the most basic elements, which go a surprisingly long way towards being a good musician. It is not necessary to be so well versed in all of the countless musical theories and principals in order to play at a high level, improvise and play with others.

You can choose to learn more specialized and higher levels of knowledge as your journey progresses. Undoubtedly, you will pick up a great deal of knowledge naturally, "automatically" by context, without much extra effort. With that in mind let's go over some truly basic yet key ideas that you can grasp right away, if you are new to music.

To start with a profound statement, let's understand that 95 percent of the popular music we listen to is essentially based on the same musical principles. In this book, I'm going to state most of those principles in layman's terms, so you formally educated types, please don't take issue.

Many of the most famous and successful musicians of modern times were not formally trained with any traditional musical education at all.

So in this light, these ideas should be all good and useful for our purposes. If I use any basic musical terms or words you don't understand they will be the more common ones you can easily lookup.

All modern popular music is comprised of the elements of rhythm, melody, and harmony. Let's look at these primary elements closer to lay the basic foundation for understanding and thereby creating a context and meaning for you to implement as you progress later on.

Rhythm is a steady beat. You can think of it like a heartbeat which, in light of music's primal origins, may be quite relevant. In a piece of music there are stronger, more emphasized beats and weaker, less emphasized beats. In essence there is a rhythmic pulse as it's termed. Most music actually weaves in and out of these beats to be more interesting and not boring or overly repetitive. The tempo or speed is also a huge element in determining the musical nature or style.

Melody is that line in a song that you either sing or hum. It is the lead musical phrase that you remember and is defined as a single line such as the voice that sings the words in your favorite song. Another trait of a melody is it likely has its own unique rhythm that complements or even counters the more regular background rhythm and beat. The melody line can be a human voice, other musical instrument, or combination.

Harmony can be defined very simply as the presence of more than one note sounded at the same time. This is different from melody which we defined as a single musical line or "voice". Harmony creates a depth or thickness in sound. When two or more notes, lines, or "voices" are played in unison, then harmony is created. Harmony can be thought of as the result of all the layers of musical notes or sounds.

Related to harmony are the basic musical elements known as chords. A chord is at its most basic form a group of usually three or more notes played simultaneously. The common musical term used is a "triad", the prefix, "tri" meaning, "three".

The concept of chords in actual practice takes us a little bit deeper into the elements of music. We want to at least understand the basics of chords and their overall significance and purpose in relation to a musical piece. In the next chapter, we will take that next step to learning the underlying basics. These will be the tools you use for making beautiful music. Let's do it together.

3

A Major Concept

To elaborate on my earlier profound statement, one remarkable thing about music is there's just one set of tonality principles that 95 percent of modern music uses. This set of principles to which I'm referring is called the diatonic system. It is the theory that defines what we commonly know as the "major scale". Oh no, here comes the complicated music theory. NOT!

Have you heard the song phrase that goes, Doe-Ray-Me-Fa-So-La-Tee-Doe? I think most of us have. it's one of the simplest universally known musical lines or vocal exercises. It's in the song from that famous musical and perhaps from your elementary school music class.

It's not really critical for you to know it, but please look it up online or ask a friend, if you haven't heard it before. Alternatively if you can manage to find a piano, starting from the middle C note play in order, on the white keys only, up to the C an octave higher. You can sing the words if you like, and it's the same song phrase.

It merely illustrates how simple the basics of music can be. The remarkable thing to know is: that little musical phrase itself, in fact, IS a perfect example of the "major scale" also known in musical terminology as the "diatonic scale". For simplicity's sake, throughout this book we often will refer to this as simply "the scale".

As simple and silly as it sounds, that simple scale is the core basic building block of probably all the music you know and love. That particular scale is only made of seven actual notes, although you may have counted eight.

The first and last notes (the "Does") are actually the "same" musical note. A musical scale just repeats the same order as you go higher (or lower) in pitch. More on that later. "The scale" is the beginning reference point for all melody notes in practically any popular song.

You can also say that the scale is a beginning reference point for all harmony notes in that song. How do I mean? Well, as mentioned briefly, a basic chord is made up of more than one note, usually three, for example. The notes in each chord also come from the same scale.

Conveniently, there is one chord that belongs to or is named for each one of the seven notes in the scale. That's the starting point of how harmony is created and implemented. More on this later.

Add the final element of rhythm, and believe it or not, you have practically all you need to begin learning and making music TODAY. When you begin to grasp these most basic, primary concepts you'll start to form a clear idea of how to use these elements creatively.

That is what we will learn step by step, so you will see how the pieces magically come together for you. After all, music is almost a kind of magic.

I already said that music is mysterious, before. A prime example and reason is that this diatonic system of notes and chords was created from long gone eras of the past. It has remained in use today, because it just plain works and has for centuries.

We really don't know all of the reasons why it works other than within the framework that we have come to know and accept. For this very reason, many famous artists such as jazz musicians have said that music IS magic, and it is the only REAL MAGIC that we know.

Regardless of WHY it works, those of us familiar with the diatonic system know the ins and outs of HOW to make it work. It has become our artistic medium. We know how we can refer to, adapt, and use it to create what we choose. Soon it will become your medium as an artist and performer.

Maybe it's not an exact science, but we can musically, artistically create the entire spectrum of human emotions using it in a spontaneous, yet surprisingly methodical way. Let's press on with adding a few more pieces to our creative musical learning.

4

Homework, It's Not Working on Your Home

Your first homework assignment is to learn a scale and some chords, and that's mostly it. This is of course a quite short book to give you the essentials, so we cannot elaborate with many deep dives into all the elements discussed. The goal is to set you on the right path with the fundamental pieces needed to go forward. Then you can take it as far as you wish with the correct focus.

With that in mind, know that you will have an edge, if you occasionally self-study and learn higher level aspects of these fundamentals. They primarily include: scales, chords, harmonies, melodies, and rhythm. At the very least you will need to learn a minimum of these basic elements of music and learn how to apply them on your instrument of choice.

Without giving you years of lessons on piano, voice, or guitar, therefore, here is the minimum that you must learn now, if you haven't already. Learn how to play on your instrument at least one major scale, (the seven scale notes). Then next, learn some chords.

Know these notes inside and out and how to play them well enough so that they become automatic. To clarify, you don't need to name them all as you play them, but just know their location or the "pattern" of where to find them on your instrument.

For example, the "pattern" to locate the seven notes of the C major scale on the piano we defined as starting at middle C note and including all the white keys only up to the next higher C note. This repeats continuously over and over. Therefore, all the white keys on the piano top to bottom are all parts or extensions of the C major scale.

You can now start to get them into your "muscle memory", i.e., your brain. Over a short learning period, you'll have them memorized and easily played. You should know how to play notes of the scale backwards and forwards, in random pieces, in small parts, or as a whole. In other words, you'll be able to find at least in random order the notes when needed.

In addition, in the near future, try to learn the seven notes of the scale in higher and lower tones (a.k.a., higher/lower octaves). As we said the seven notes repeat in the same order as we go to higher or lower ranges (octaves).

As we discussed a major scale is the "Doe-Ray-Me…" phrase. You can sound that out and find those notes on your instrument, if needed. If it's the piano, then I suggest the C major scale as I described in the earlier section. Otherwise, it's easy enough to find how to play any major scale from online or from a basic book on how to play major scales.

The names of scale notes are alphabetical but in music we use only the letters A through G, (seven total), then the letters A through G repeat again, continuously in a loop.

In any scale you choose which note to start on first. It could be C as we noted above, or it could be G, or A. Whichever letter name it is will also be what's known as the tonal center. This tonal center note is often referred to as your home base. It is the note probably most often played in a song, for example, it is usually the first as well as last note played in a song.

The tonal center is a very valuable piece of information and concept, so we will elaborate. With the C major scale as our chosen "key". If we then choose the tonal center to be A, we will still use all of the same seven scale notes we've already identified as the C scale.

However, the entire nature of the sound will change dramatically. The mood and style of the music will be very different, and we will explain later. Just know that this is part of the resource in musical vocabulary you've already begun to build.

The next step is to learn how to play some chords of our major scale. As stated, there are actually seven chords that accompany a major scale, one for each scale note, but you can start by knowing just a few chords and learn the rest at your leisure as you get more experience.

Incidentally, if your singing voice is your instrument of choice, then you won't learn to sound chords, but chord knowledge will serve you when singing with other instruments or other vocalists. The next section will explain more details of the chords you need to learn.

5

More on Chords, More or Less

How to create the chords from a major scale is fairly simple. You start with defining your chosen major scale. If the first note of your chosen major scale is C then, the scale is called the C major scale. The seven notes (which repeat) would then be C-D-E-F-G-A-B-C. Remember that in a musical scale, the last note is a repeat of the first note, and then the scale repeats in the same order over and over.

There is a chord for each note of the scale, in other words a chord built upon each scale note as we've stated. Therefore there is a C chord, a D chord, an E chord, etc..

Here is how building chords on each note works: The chords we are going to build will each have three notes. The first note is the chord name, ex., C chord has its first note of C, then skip every other note of the scale to choose the next note(s), i.e., the second and third notes of the chord. In other words, the C chord is made up of these three notes: C,E,G. The D chord is made up of these three notes: D,F,A.

An integral, related concept is that when you play all seven chords of the scale in order, it's known as the harmonized scale. As the name implies, we're beginning to get into the subject of harmony, which we'll touch on more later. Knowing how the chords fit into our system is a fundamental part of the process, and we'll learn to actually use and apply this knowledge.

The seven chords derived from the scale are each named by the scale note's name. The scale note and its chord are also named using Roman Numerals. Therefore, instead of using letter names, they are also referred to as the I, II, III. IV, V, VI, and VII notes, degrees, or chords. These terms then refer to the I chord or degree, or V chord or degree. This is useful when we have different letter names for the different scales and therefore names for the chords.

Also, you must understand there are different types of chords, mainly we will limit our discussion to two types known as "major" and "minor" chords.

An important principle to learn is that the I, IV, and V chords are always major type chords. The II, III, and VI chords are always minor type chords. The VII is a lesser used type of chord known as half diminished, but we won't need to know or use that for now.

Therefore, to be more accurate, in the C major scale, above, the seven TRUE chord names (and their Roman numeral symbols) in practice are as follows: C major (I), D minor (ii), E minor (iii), F major (IV), G major (V), A minor (vi), B Half Diminished (vii).

The proper chord names and types will have more meaning when learning to actually play them. The proper names are important also, if you wish to look them up online or from a book of chords, for example.

6

Context of Songs. They're Good

With these conceptual tools in the bag, let's now begin to really get into our music creation approach and method. To do so we'll keep our purpose and objective in mind.

Therefore, it will be best for our learning process to set the context in the form of learning and playing songs. Learning to put together songs, melodies, and harmonies using the musical elements we've discussed will be the most effective and efficient approach.

This is a process to get us where we want to be in the most meaningful and efficient way. Ultimately, you will not be limited to just learning familiar songs, since the same principals and techniques will apply to all musical adaptations, i.e., improvising, song composing, and song arranging, for example.

To start, choose a song that you perhaps listen to and like, and then begin to learn to play it with the guidelines that follow. Alternatively, you may wish to create and compose your own song right away. It may prove much more challenging, if you are new to music, but it's not out of the question.

Let's presume that we are learning a particular song familiar to you. It's an easy shortcut, especially these days, to first find the written music online or from a music book if you have it. Note, however, you won't actually need to know how to read music notation.

We really just want to pull some basic information we mentioned, which is some or part of the melody and the some or all of the chords. That is what we will mainly try to get from a piece of sheet music or other chart, if available. The process can be highly simplified by having this, but we can still go without, if needed.

We most likely are already familiar enough with the sound of the melody whether vocal or instrumental and how it sounds in our head. We can start by focusing on just one line of the verse or line of the chorus. Also we want to learn how to play some or most of the chords used in the song.

One suggestion at the start is to find a song that does not have many chords in it, maybe just a handful 3-4, or less. As you begin learning this will make it easier, and later as you gain more experience you won't need to worry about a chord limit.

If at all possible, I'd suggest an internet search for the song name and add the search term "chords" and the instrument of your choice if you like. Once we have the chords and or music chart, then we have all we really need plus some helpful information to make it easier.

If you don't know much musical notation or recognize chords, just find and learn the letter names of the chords. Note: you don't always need to play a chord at all times or exactly as it's written either. It will be your decision how often. As we'll learn in the next section of musical arranging it's your own arrangement after all.

Mostly you are concerned with the main melody line and simply embellishing it when you feel it is best or when the song occasionally requires you to. To take a step back, that statement may seem very unlike what you expected.

If you've ever had music lessons, this is probably very different from the way you were traditionally instructed or how a typical lesson, instruction book reads. That is because in our more creative, artistic, and individual approach to music we are now touching on the subject of musical arrangement.

Musical Arrangement:

Creating an arrangement or "arranging music" is a concept that means you can choose the instruments, the rhythm, how the individual parts of the song go, and what the actual melodies and harmonies are. In other words you can follow the original song, change it slightly, or completely reinvent it to suit your preferences or tastes.

Therefore, with some very basic musical choices you are right away establishing your own style, becoming more creative and intuitive. Even a beginner can take this on, and trust me, you'll be glad when you realize its immediate effect on your learning and the content of your performance.

This is also where the real enjoyment, creativity, and even genius can emerge. Yes it can, even at the early stages of learning. This also defines the way I'll be teaching you to view and learn songs. Taking this approach is what makes this method different from many traditional ways of learning music. Staying mindful of this will make the entire process more constructive, creative and enjoyable.

At its heart arranging is the art of giving an existing melody musical variety. We will keep it simple to start, but just know that as you learn more, this process can be very rewarding and one of the most exciting aspects of music for both you and your audience.

You can always stick to the original version and try to duplicate or emulate it. However, as mentioned, by making different creative choices, your musical knowledge and resourcefulness will greatly expand. Very quickly your resulting performances will begin to reflect it.

7

The Key is the Key

L et's get back to the drawing board. Now, there is one starting point for learning a song that can prove to be a bit tricky. With practice you will get more proficient at it though. This involves finding the key, or major scale of choice.

We need to choose one scale that we want to use for our song. In layman's terms the key is the group or pool of notes that you will pull from to play the melody, the harmony and also to create all other tonality related parts of the song.

The major key or scale choice will depend on a few factors. Do you wish to play the original key, another version, or your own interpretation? This can be a personal choice or it may depend on whether the melody can be comfortably sung or played by you, for example.

Often it is beneficial to find out what the key of the song is as originally written, then you can easily change to another key, if you wish. As mentioned, you at least need to learn one major scale, and your song choice will likely affect what scale you should learn.

As you gain experience, you will have all of the scales or keys available to you, if you don't already know them. Note that all the major scales behave in the exact same way, but just have a different starting note and letter name. In general, any chosen key can be used for any song by "transposing" or "converting" all of the song notes and chords to another key.

Some tips to determine the key of a song as it is written are: If you are familiar with key signatures, then you can simply read it from the staff lines on the music sheet. This is a good item for you to add to your to do list for future learning. Therefore, you can easily recognize the key as it is written on a piece of music.

The first melody note, the first chord and/or the last chord played are usually the tonal center and possibly the same as the key of the song. Remember that there is a difference between the definition of the major key and the tonal center. They can be the same but are not necessarily.

Look at the different chord types used in the song to give you a clue. Hopefully you chose a song to start with only a with few chords in it. As discussed before, in any one key the I, IV, and V chords are the major type chords. The II, III, and VI are the minor type chords. Take a close look and see which chords correlate with these types. With a little effort and bit of reasoning, you'll be able to determine which is the I chord, IV chord, etc..

One note is that these rules are often broken and only major chords are used, for example, sometimes because, "it's good enough for rock and roll". Regardless, what you determine to be the I chord is also the name of your major key.

The original key also may be noted somewhere on the chart. If not, then you may also be able to do a web search to find it out.

As mentioned, you may choose a key other than the original. Therefore, to change keys from one to another, you can simply rename the chords with the appropriate Roman numerals, including the chord types. Then from the original key correlate the Roman numerals/chord types with those of the key you want to use instead.

Alternatively find the distance between the I chord of the original key and the I chord of your desired key. For example it may be three half steps from C down to A. You can then take that same distance, three half steps, to convert every note and chord from one key to the next. In this case the result is changing the key of C major to A major.

Foundational Ideas:

Once you have chosen the key, and major scale work out how to play the melody or just some parts of it. You can either get help or clues from the music sheet or do it by ear.

Play it by using only the notes of the scale that you've previously learned on your instrument. The melody should not stray from these seven notes other than in higher registers or octaves. All notes will remain in your scale and not stray much at all, only very rarely.

For example, if you chose the key of C major, then on the piano all notes will be on the white keys only. All the white keys and only the white keys are the notes from the C major scale whether on the extreme high or extreme low range.

Start slowly, and you'll realize that you will have the capacity to do this, by just knowing a single major scale and using your familiarity with how the melody sounds.

Working out the melody when also playing the accompanying chords can help guide you, because you'll be better able to hear how the notes fit in with the chords played at the right time.

Just sound the chords in the general place that you hear them fitting into the song. Depending on how much notation you know, the music sheet you referenced may also make it easier to find the melody notes on your instrument.

Remember that this is an intuitive process and not highly technical. In addition, along with the melody, try to find any signature notes, lines or distinctive, familiar sounds of the song that you want to include. You can slightly alter them to suit your preference or just to make them easier to play. These will also not stray from you scale notes, only rarely. We will explain more on why this is so, later on.

8

Just Beat It

Besides the key lessons of melody and harmony that we've just learned, a primary element to consider should be the rhythm and tempo of the song. This is a vital part of the basic framework we want to establish. The rhythm choice may greatly determine the resulting musical style or genre of any piece.

A rhythmic pulse is an essential element upon which to build your song and keep you connected from beginning to end. You can play all the right notes, but if they're not tied together and synced to an underlying rhythm, then it won't sound quite right.

Feel the strong beats and weak beats. It's easiest at the start to choose a song with 4/4 time signature. If not, you can still think in the terms of 4 beats at a time. Practice counting 1,2,3,4.

Regularly play a bass, or low note(s) or other signature note(s), melody note(s) on the 1&3 beats. On guitar, I like to play a lower, bass note with my thumb or slight down stroke on these strong beats.

On the 2&4 beats regularly play a percussive style of a strum, a pluck, strike on the keyboard, for example. I like to consistently create this "back beat" with a sharp down stroke on the guitar.

The sensing of the beat will come through and enhance your music in the ears of both you and the listener. In other words, the notes and chords that you play should take on a rhythmic, percussive quality at times.

The resulting combination of sounds will have more context and meaning within the performance. This subtle difference will make a very meaningful change in the quality of your music.

You may want to start at half speed and slow the tempo to make things easier. As your coordination, dexterity and skills improve you'll speed it up. The techniques for creating an underlying rhythm don't need to be complicated. A very simple bass line can be a single note or just a concerted effort to use your instrument's most basic strumming, plucking, or other methods.

For example, if you play the piano, then consider that your left hand will be in charge of the bass and rhythm elements more so than your right hand which will play more of the melody or signature line parts. On a guitar your strumming hand will be the one in charge of creating a clear rhythm and your fretting hand will be the one in charge of the notes.

Always be aware of the rhythmic elements in your playing. Aim to hear your own preferences in rhythm. Make your own rhythmic choices within the framework of your chosen song. You will find yourself getting better with practice, both in perception and in conveying rhythms with your own distinctive style.

The rhythmic element is often a result of or characteristic of your chosen instrument. As we've discussed, the actual physical motions you use can take an almost percussive or drum like characteristic, in fact. If you are a singer, keep a steady pulse and beat with simple tapping motions of your feet, hands or use of tambourine or maraca, if possible.

For example, feel as if you are "slapping" a down stroke of your guitar strings on the strong beats or "banging" emphatically on the keys of the piano. Famous musicians may come to mind such as Stanley Jordan and Jimi Hendrix on guitar or Jerry Lee Lewis and Billy Joel on the piano.

Be highly aware of the underlying rhythmic pulse. Do so in ways we've described, and you will figuratively and musically create your own drum set within a song. By regularly stressing the 1&3 beats it's akin to the bass drum in the form of a bass note or percussive stroke. On the back beats or 2&4, your chord and/or stroke is like the part of a snare drum.

Fill in the smaller subdivisions of beats with some lighter, softer dynamic ,random, fill notes, from your scale. These are akin to the high hat cymbal, and will spatially fill out the overall sound.

You will keep better musical time as another added benefit. Think of the larger beats as the minutes of a clock and the smaller fractions of beats like the ticking seconds between. Randomly fill them with notes and chords tied together to the pulsing beat.

All Together Now:

What we've tried to set forth in our approach is a melodic, rhythmic, and textured effect in playing and arranging music. The overall effect we want to achieve is for the different parts, rhythms, and voices to spontaneously create their own texture and therefore become their own arrangement.

One of the best and simplest arrangement methods to use is to play a few bass notes, a predetermined bass line or very simple improvised one, then combine it with just the melody lines or signature notes. Those two parts alone will usually sound great. You can use this method for an entire song or for certain sections. It's at least a technique for variation that you have at your command whenever needed.

This arranging concept is not based on a lot of technical musical knowledge, but just the interplay, complement, and contrast of two "independent" parts. It has a powerful effect when your ears hear the separate parts intertwined.

This creates great interest in the listener's ear as well making it a very powerful and simple technique. Often it has the effect of the listener thinking you are doing something much more difficult than you really are.

With the rhythm in mind and also knowing the major scale notes and chords you will fill in the space around the bass, melody, and other signature notes. This is a very spontaneous, creative, and intuitive way to perform that musicians of almost any level can learn to apply.

One of the most often used techniques involves finding areas within a song or a performance where there are no melody notes being played. This is where you add almost "mini solos" or "micro-improvisations". They may only be a few notes added within a few beats of a measure.

It could be at the end of each measure or short musical phrase and repeated several times in a row.

They may be a question and answer type of interplay where a small line or musical motif is played or sung by one player. Moments later it is answered by another player with a similar or variation of that sound or motif. As mentioned we are adding to the texture and filling the space between bass notes, melodies, and signature notes. We are embellishing the song when we occasionally add small touches where and when we see fit.

There is one other great benefit to incorporating this melodic, rhythmic, and textured effect in playing and arranging your music. Your music and sound will stand on its own very well without anyone else helping or accompanying you.

Your style will have the elements of what is known as a "solo performer style". This means you are almost like a one person band, because you have created several parts within your piece of music. This can all be done with a single instrument. If you also sing, then that's a bonus, since you'll have another part to add, and we'll discuss the whole other dimension of singing later.

You have created an instrumental bass and rhythm part with chords, and you've filled in lead parts with signature lines and partial melodies. Although you're always able to play with others and tailor to a group dynamic, you can play music quite well on your own.

You are creating much more than a single part because you now know how to. As a friend and mentor of mine who is a solo performer says, it's good for the soul. It's very gratifying to perform and create a "complete song" in this style. Other than that just do it because you can.

9

Work It. It Works

So far what we've covered is the basic framework of how to approach a piece of music using the core elements of melody and harmony while never forgetting to mention rhythm as well. Instrumentally this is only possible when we are equipped with the basic knowledge of the major scale and a few chords that fit the particular scale and song.

The process gives us the ability to navigate learning a song, arranging it to our liking or to an agreed upon version of the song when played together with other musicians.

Through learning this process in the context of a song, moreover, we will have gained the ability to improvise or solo within a song or random session with fellow musicians.

Over a short period of time and into the long term with experience, we will develop favorite riffs, signature lines, and our own tricks. The skills and resources for you to draw upon will naturally grow and evolve by sharing with peers and doing some of your own research and development.

Ultimately, if we choose, we will also be able to use these techniques and resources in our own musical composition endeavors. Take your creativity to the next level and it will surely be satisfying for you.

Let's go a bit deeper now to further understand the ways we can use the tools we've learned so far. The tools to which I am referring are the major scale and the accompanying chords. If we have a better understanding of what they really represent, we'll have the ability to make greater use of them towards our musical and artistic goals or objectives.

A Deeper Dive:

The real heart of the material we've discussed so far is the tonality created by use of a scale and accompanying chords. By definition in musical terms, tonality refers to the character of a piece of music based on its key or on the relation of its tones and chords to a particular key note.

We have a melody or main line of the song as well as some signature lines or mini melodies within, you might say. The chords are used not only to create harmonies, but as a more rhythmic element. They are a background upon which to play the single melodic lines and signature notes or lines.

The overall concept that brings these elements together goes back to the chosen key and its accompanying chords. As we discussed earlier the key or major scale notes are the group of notes we draw from. To take this a step deeper we should know that we use this and only this group of notes for every musical line, phrase or sound within a song.

As it happens to work out, all of the notes from each chord (three or more notes per chord) are ALSO from the same group of notes of the scale or key. That is because we created each chord directly from the chosen scale as you should recall.

By adhering to the simple principle of staying in key, it makes all the different notes played and all the chords played fit together and sound pleasing to the ear. The notes do not clash, which in musical terms is called dissonance. The overall effect, therefore, doesn't sound like random noise and unpleasing to the ear.

As you may recall, I briefly spoke of how this system has been around for centuries and it just works as we have come to know and accept it. We can't always explain why it works so well, but we do know how to abide by these rules of tonality and staying "in the key".

As far as the subject of tonality goes, or notes being connected in key and sounding good to the ear, we now have the magic formula to create good sounding music. In fact we have countless options and the ability to artistically create as we play music in almost any style or way we choose.

10

Freedom of Choice

We have virtual musical freedom to play any note at any time while playing any chord at any time. It can be completely random and an infinite variety of "in key" melodies and harmonies will be created.

An additional benefit of this way of arranging the music to your liking is that you will not need to spend weeks perfecting a single song note by note. You can learn a tune much faster as you get used to the process. You can learn many more songs and do it faster, I'd even say better in many ways.

You can actually learn to play a song immediately with just a few chords and create the music as you play it. I personally love this process for this reason. I'm always creating on the fly as I play and in fact, will rarely play a song the same exact way twice. Doesn't that sound like fun? It is.

All we need to do for this to succeed is stick to using only the group of notes that are in a particular key or major scale. Whether the notes used are single notes or chords made up of several notes doesn't matter for the formula to work. Most musicians know this intuitively, but may have had it taught to them with more technical terms and methods.

Those not familiar with this aspect of music "language" are baffled completely and think its more complex than it really is. Anyone with average or perhaps below average musical ability can make a huge leap in progress armed with this insight and with just a reasonable amount of effort.

The process outlined above is also a good way to describe the activity of improvisation. In musical circles this is also called "jamming", "free form improv", and is also how "soloing" is performed when one instrument creates a lead instrumental line on the spot, in the moment, and out of the blue.

The guitarist, the saxophone, the piano, and any other player can all take their turn at soloing in a song because they are on the same page with each other and playing in the same key. Here is where a band's live performance chemistry of the musicians emerges.

An instrumental solo or even a vocal solo is performed and created off the top of one's head or spontaneously. What the soloist must keep in mind is the particular tonality, "key" or "scale" notes that will work in a given context or over a given musical "backdrop". The backdrop in turn is made up of one or more accompaniments such as other instruments also playing the chords and/or notes of that key.

A prime example of tonality "in key" was mentioned prior as the "harmonized scale" made up of all the seven chords over a major scale. These chords can actually be played just as the individual notes of the scale are, in a random sequence order or in a "chord solo", if you will. This is a powerful musical tool to use and a very unique, creative approach as compared to simply following the chords exactly as written on paper.

Blueprint for Success:

The basics that we've learned are the foundation and blueprint that this book is meant to teach. In such a short book, we cannot include all the more detailed applications of these lessons. Those would include ideas such as extended harmonies, non harmonic melody tones, extended chords and chord progressions.

The more technical aspects and higher level subtleties can be learned independently. This will depend on your specific preferences and areas of interest as needed.

Musical skill development in any sense will always be an ongoing, continuous journey of learning and discovery. I only wish to steer you in the right direction, so you won't need to go deeper into technical, complex ideas any more than needed.

As mentioned earlier on, it will always help you to get an edge and learn more of these topics: chord structure and use, chord progressions, melody writing, lyric writing, modal harmonies, voice training, rhythmic elements and styles.

With the core knowledge we've covered, you have the tools to expand into playing in groups with others and also the ability to compose original material. For these are both applications of the same principles of key tonality with notes and chords.

11

Composed. Cool and...

How do these principles now apply if you were going to compose original music? The basics are essentially the same. You need a melody and a key that are based on the ideas of tonality and chord elements we outlined in the previous chapters.

There are key ideas that go just a bit deeper that will definitely help you become a composer of music as compared to only relying on existing works. Not that there is anything wrong with that.

After all, many many great songs are out there, and why not play them for the enjoyment of others as well as your own satisfaction. Besides, in the way I've taught in this book, the approach is highly creative and quite original in its own way. You'll actually begin to make others' songs your own with your own arrangements and unique style.

A simple way to think of composing original music is that you are reverse engineering, if you will. When you were learning to play a familiar song, the chords and notes of the scale helped to guide you in playing the song you already knew in your head. Now you need to use the same tools to create your own original song that works as a whole. Therefore, there are some key ideas we need to touch on to know how to go about it.

One main idea is called "song form". Typically in popular music especially, there will be verses and choruses. Think of the verse as the beginning of a song that gets introduces the listener slowly to the upcoming musical melodies or phrases. The chorus is the part that is repeated often with more power or feeling. The chorus is the most memorable phrase of the song, and often contains the actual song title in its words.

Each section of a song can be referred to as part A, or part B. Therefore, common song forms are the ABA or the AABA form. For example, the A section is played once, then the B section and returning to the A section (ABA). A section can be any length, but typically it will be 4 to 8 measures.

As we stated before, in general, you can play any chord and any melody or signature note(s) at any time, in sync with some form of rhythm of course. The random combinations of sound combine okay as long as they come from the same pool of available notes.

What represents those notes is the chosen major scale or key. Therefore, one of the main if not first step is to choose a key. You may change it later, but stick with one for now so you can formulate and refine your ideas in a framework that you've learned already.

There is no set rule on how to spark your creative process. You may start with a melody, or with some chords, or even an abstract idea, mood, or intended effect is what works. However, we'll go over the key elements, then you can apply them when you need to.

Coming up with a new melody is probably one of the most spontaneous processes. There are not a lot of specific steps to it other than sticking with the notes of your chosen scale. Melodies may come easy to you in your head, or they may take more trial and error to find one that sticks and is memorable.

Find inspiration in songs that you like, or feelings and images that you'd like to capture. Without getting too philosophical, music as an art and art is like life. One description of art is that it is an objective representation of a subjective event. How would you choose to make your listener or even yourself connect to that subjective event through your music? Is the quality perhaps how well you accomplish this task? A bit deep for this book, I know. I think you should dive deep and enjoy it.

Keep in mind that these melody notes will coincide and blend with the chords. Therefore if you have one or more chords selected, try to use many of the notes that each chord contains.

No one can tell you which chords to include in your song or how many for that matter. Maybe you just want one chord, or none. You'll need to identify what types of chords may work for you. Remember that there are the seven chords that belong to any major scale.

As we said in the beginning, we don't always know exactly why some musical ideas work so well, but have accepted them because they just do. It's magic that works, at least in the context of popular music that we know. Over time it has evolved in our societies and cultures.

There are some very well known progressions that simply work well and have been used repeatedly throughout musical history. We won't dive into the intricate details of why the chord notes within certain chords create diatonic relationships and dynamics in progressions, that's a mouthful already.

Basically we want to learn about the best order of chords to play. The concept of chord progressions describes the way that certain chord groups in certain sequences are inherently more effective than others.

To begin, choose one or more chords as a background against which to play and perhaps solo or try out ideas. Some common very strong progressions are: I-IV-V or ii-V-I or I-V-I or just I. You don't have to follow any strict rules, but these combinations or sequences of chords are known to work well.

Try them out, and see if they peak your interest. For example, to emulate one of your favorite songs, then perhaps look at some of the progressions used, (Roman numeral symbols-wise), and incorporate them into your own work.

Another very powerful chord progression to learn is the V-I. This is one of the most useful and effective combinations. It's a great way to end a song as the I chord is your home base. The V chord contains certain diatonic elements that create a strong pull towards the I chord.

Without going too deep, the distance between scale notes, is called an "interval". The interval distance between the I and the V note is called an interval of a "fifth". There is in fact a well known theory known as the "Circle of Fifths" based on this V-I relationship. In a nutshell you can always precede any chord with its relative V chord. In other words, if

39

the chords are are a fifth apart then the progression works and sounds good. Take the time to look it up, as stated we won't go into all the details.

Let's now combine the melody notes with the chords or vice versa. The notes of your original melody or signature lines need to sound good with the chords used. One basic way to make them do so is to emphasize one of the three notes of a chord. That is, when a certain chord is played, also play one of the three notes of that chord as a part of your melody or musical phrase or line.

Of course, you can always play any single melody note at any time when the chords are also in key. However, by emphasizing the chord notes simultaneously at chosen times of a song (ex., strong beats 1&3) it is sure to create a strong blend of chord and melody.

Also be aware of the types of chords that you use. We outlined the two main types of chords as major and minor. Over time, make an effort to learn more about chord types, since there are many variations and other types.

Remember the true chord types that we outlined in the beginning section on chords. In the major key of C, the chords that you will use are: C major, D minor, E minor, F major, G major, A minor, and B half diminished.

In general, major types of chords create feelings of happiness, and are more upbeat. Minor types of chords create feelings of more sadness, or deeper feelings. As musical artists we will want to create and apply elements of emotion, mood, and "lifelike" experience. This is just one piece that will help to understand how to use the tools for your musical intent or inspiration.

This brings us to a topic we touched on earlier. That is tonal center and how to make use of it for creating a variety of moods, feelings, and styles. As stated, if the major key is C for example, then the seven notes of the scale are C-D-E-F-G-A-B.

If C is also our tonal center, then a major type of scale and tonality results. A major tonality as we stated is generally associated with a happy, upbeat, feeling. The music we create with this tonal center will have this positive, upbeat mood and overall feeling.

In contrast, if we still use the key of C major, but choose the tonal center to be A, we now have a different scale because the order of notes is now A-B-C-D-E-F-G. This is a minor type of scale. A minor scale creates feelings that are deeper, or more sad compared to a major scale. You can try it out on a piano, keeping to the white keys, and hear the change.

In our given key of C major, this choice creates the distinctive A minor sound versus the C major sound. This is one of the most often used alternate choices of tonal center. For your reference, the A is the VI degree of our major scale, as compared to C which is the I degree, as you'll recall.

Therefore, you can choose from seven different tonal centers when in the key of C major. Each one creates a unique sound and style. The resulting "scales" from each of the tonal centers are termed "modes". I won't go into them in depth, and you can dive deeper into the names and uses on your own. I do highly recommend you use them all as they are useful in many styles of music from jazz, rock, fusion, classical and bossa nova.

For the purposes of this book, just know that these rich resources of music all come from the simple major scale. You can use this concept in a variety of ways. You can switch tonal centers in the middle of your instrumental solo for added variety. You can choose to compose happier songs or deeper feeling songs by your choice of tonal center and the resulting major or minor tonalities created.

12

No Paralysis by Analysis

The idea of musical arranging that we discussed earlier is highly relevant in original composing. The instruments chosen, the lead parts, rhythm, harmonies, tonal centers and all of the stylistic musical choices are yours to make. You can follow all the known "rules" or none of them. Use all your musical tools and knowledge simply as resources to draw upon as needed.

An overall statement I'd like to make at this point is that what we've learned so far is just enough technical know how to begin applying it. There are countless aspects of these basics that we cannot go into in this short book and are not yet useful in a practical way. If we get too analytical in our process we'll suffer from paralysis by analysis.

For instance, all you practically need to know is that by staying with only the notes of your chosen major scale and only the chords that we've outlined, you have all the music rules you need. Yes, this gives you certain guidelines to stay within, but it also gives you a whole lot of freedom to create, improvise and take control of the process. You can create your own style, mood, and dynamics as you choose. It was when I realized this, that my playing was completely liberated. I stopped overthinking everything and my playing took a giant leap. I had free reign to let go and like Steely Dan says, "play just what I feel".

You do not need to analyze every harmonic, tonal or intervallic relationship you are creating. Most are random and you're just feeling out things as you hear them. Later on you can take the time to see why something technically works well or not, but it may not even matter.

Hone your skill as a player by doing what works and experimenting and taking chances. You can accelerate your growth as a performer by going with your gut feelings and relying on your ever growing experience.

Those well versed in modern jazz will identify with this spontaneous and free form type of musical expression. In many other genres as well, you can observe this in live musical performances, for instance.

Most rock and pop musicians are actively creating new phrasing, solos and arrangements when they perform live. Do you notice that they often don't try to duplicate their songs note for note? Instead they know the basic framework of a given song, and then they take liberties and even musical risks when performing.

Great musicians enjoy this, because it's freeing and empowering. It's also what a live audience really wants to see in a good performance, not merely an exact duplication of a recorded version. With experience you will come to enjoy this process in the same way, no matter what skill level you are currently.

13

This Bird Can Sing. It's in the Words

I f you want to be a singer, you can. I'll go over some of the keys to get there. If you want to compose, then you'll want to begin writing your own vocal melodies and lyrics.

Writing your own lyrics is also a broad topic you should explore on your own. It can be highly individualistic and unlimited in it's variety and style. If needed, there are many resources available such as books and other media on the topic of lyric writing.

Matching the words to music is often a very intuitive process. You will most often adapt a line to the melody or vice versa, and it doesn't need to be too technical. The underlying rhythm of the music will match up at least roughly to the meter of your writing. With trial and error you'll adapt each to the other, as needed.

Let's discuss some of the keys to gain skill in singing. To start with, the human voice in popular music has it's advantages and disadvantages compared to other musical instruments. It is certainly a great way to come up with a melody either by singing or humming it at first.

In more technical musical aspects, vocal melodies may need to be more simple in their nature than a fast, multi-octave range, saxophone or guitar solo, for example. The vocal phrases won't include very rapid changes or extreme leaps in pitch from the very lowest to very highest.

These kinds of dynamics are too much strain and not as easily done as they are with many instruments . Notes and phrases are often repeated more in a vocal line, and are not complex, especially in the chorus section of a song.

In some ways the voice is not as dynamic or ornamented as many musical instruments. On the other hand, the voice can actually fuse, bend, and shape musical sounds in ways the more mechanical instruments cannot. It's been said that the saxophone is the instrument that most closely resembles the singing voice.

Every voice is unique and at its heart a personal, human touch brought into our art form. In its unique way, the voice can convey the most powerful and memorable feelings. Don't shy away from it. If you have it, use it, and I believe we all can.

Most if not all of us have adequate singing ability, regardless of what you may think. Anyone can at least get to an average level of singing quality, and you'll be thrilled when you find yourself going beyond what you expected and more.

I'll give you various tips from my learning and musical experience in the following sections. The main advice I'll give is to stay in your own vocal range. Most of us are not gifted with an unusually high or wide vocal range, which then leads to the belief that we have no singing talent. I'm here to tell you that is absolutely wrong, and you do have the ability to sing with great skill. How to do it begins simply by singing within your given vocal range. Perfecting and refining your skills can come later and will with experience.

Therefore, to find out what your range is try to sing along with a piano or other instrument. For example, start on middle C of the piano and try to sing it. Go up the keyboard one note at a time trying to sing each one. When your voice strains or needs to use the falsetto ("artificial") range, then that's your highest note, and that's your limit. In other words that note, (or maybe one step lower), is the highest note you can comfortably sing with sufficient volume and power.

Although you may wish to push your limit at times, and it can have a great effect, it will be hard to sustain or repeat it if too frequent. Once you know your limit, you can confidently sing your highest note, with volume, not over strain and sound good in a musical setting.

If the song you are playing or singing goes too high, (or low), then you'll need to either change the key to fit your vocal range and/or change the octave, i.e., how high or low that you sing it.

Another aspect to singing is how you control your breathing. Learn to use your breathing correctly so not to sound too "breathy" and also to not struggle to breathe. There is no need to forcefully push out the notes and that is actually detrimental to the quality of your vocal performance not to mention physical wear on your instrument. The diaphragm region evenly controls the exhaling process, and by being aware of this you'll better avoid the aforementioned mistake.

There are certain areas of the head, nasal and windpipe airways, as well as the chest and diaphragm that require focus when singing. The vocal chords and airways that produce your voice need to resonate effectively to produce your best voice quality. This is getting more into the finer aspects of singing you'll benefit from learning later on.

The voice as a musical instrument should be understood to know what you may or may not be capable of singing. You must know where your vocal range is. What are the highest and lowest notes can you sing comfortably without straining your vocal chords. If you don't identify this, and it is occurring, then you will not sound good. Others will hear and feel your strain as well.

Related to that, there is actually a sweet spot in your range that is slightly "pushing it" but not too far. If you can find this "middle" range in your voice you will optimize the dynamics, passion, and overall effectiveness of your singing voice. The inclusion of human emotion, power, and even being "on edge" all contribute to having a great musical voice.

All the many aspects and lessons regarding singing are beyond the scope of this book. However, you can learn plenty on your own, and it's likely not anywhere near difficult as you think. Take the time to self educate with a book or short lesson to use your voice in a healthy way, most importantly, and gain confidence in knowing the musical instrument that is your voice.

With some practice and by staying in your range, you'll get better at hitting musical notes with the needed accuracy of tone and vibrato or resonance. That is what will naturally improve and make the difference in your singing quality. Also with practice, you will improve power in volume, rhythm and timing.

Remember that you can arrange any song to your liking and to your own vocal range. You do have the ability sing in the context of popular music and even beyond. It takes just a minimal amount of dedicated effort and knowing the key ideas to focus on.

14

Summary & Conclusion, In That Order

And with that we are arriving at the end of our short journey. We've learned some ideas in music that may have been new to you. The overall concept of music we've outlined may be very different, especially if you've never been exposed to music theory in school or in lessons.

Even if you have some musical education, it may be a change from how you once perceived things. If so, that's progress, as long as I succeeded in helping you understand how the overall concepts work on a very practical level and what they mean to you as a creative musician and performer. The technical aspects and theories are less important in the context of this book. There was a minimal amount for you to digest, but you'll get a much deeper understanding of the musical concepts while you actively apply them.

You don't need to know everything there is to know before taking real steps to playing and creating your music. I've tried to simplify the approach to making music without formal training or lessons. With the basic foundation of ideas for you to follow you will branch out your knowledge to what you specifically wish to focus on.

To briefly summarize the main action points, we went over the following:

Start with a song you know and choose a verse, chorus or simple part. Learn 2-4 of the main chords and repeat. The song can be modified as such.

Determine the major key and/or the tonal center and differentiate between the two. Usually a big clue is the 1st chord and last chord.

Know the major scale and learn one to start. Learn the notes on your instrument so you know the patterns or other cues to find them.

The song you choose may influence the song key and major scale you learn. You'll want to transpose or "convert" the song if they are not the same key and major scale.

Choose one or more chords as a background to play/solo against. Some common progressions are : I, IV, V or ii, V, I or I, V or just I.

Start by slowing down the tempo of a song, ½ speed for example. Speed up as time goes by and your skills and dexterity improve.

Fill in the space around the bass, melody, signature note(s) with more scale notes and rhythmic elements.

The different parts, rhythms, voices, randomly, textured, become their own arrangement.

Musical sounds will emerge over time without technical knowledge and the complexity of written notation.

Rhythm is vital – know the strong beats and subdivisions. Choose a 4/4 song preferably. Practice counting 1,2,3,4. Play a lower bass note(s) or other melody,signature note(s) on beats of 1&3; alternately create a back beat on the 2&4 with chords and percussive touches or techniques.

Know the chords, particularly the harmonized scale. The main chord types are mentioned. Learn more on your own as needed to at least include these ideas: Major, minor, Dominant 7th, symbolic notation and chord degrees.

We learned of the elements needed to compose your own music. Much of the same elements used in the context of learning a song applied with some added deeper dive into some.

Finally, we learned of how you can be a better singer, to use your given vocal range. Combining the other musical elements with a voice is a unique and powerful area in music I encourage everyone to take on.

In conclusion, it is my hope that you may have seen things in a different light when it comes to making your own music. You may have realized that you or anyone else that wants has the ability to be a musician, and potentially a great one. You may find a larger perspective. You may spark a special interest that leads to your own unique style and impact. You may agree that music is a wonderful gift in which all of us can participate in a meaningful way.

You now have real tools and steps you can take immediately to get you going. I encourage you to learn as much as you can on your own to get farther, faster in your overall progress.

These basics are easily applicable to all musical styles, of course. The styles and preferences are yours whether vocal, jazz, standards, swing, bossa nova, rock or pop.

I personally enjoy a very wide variety of musical genres. I can appreciate all music more so , since I've learned many of the aspects in this book of how it really works. The genres and styles may differ greatly, but they have a lot of elements in common like those we discussed.

In my own performances, I feel strongly influenced by rock, jazz, perhaps blues and R&B. As for my all time influences and favorite songs to play it's a lot of '60s and '70s rock.

On that note, as John Lennon said:

"Music is everybody's possession. It's only publishers who think that people own it."

I like the following common UK expression, and so adding my best British accent, my only quote is , "Just get on with it then, eh?!?"

Also by DDJ Publishing

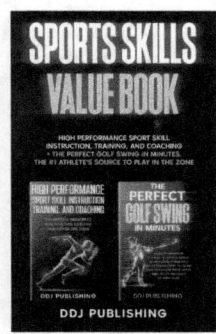

SPORTS SKILLS VALUE BOOK

High Performance Sport Skill Instruction, Training, and Coaching

Every sportsperson seeks the elusive next level up. Whether at the pro or beginner level there are hidden, inner sources of power to improve and excel.

Famous, three-time Grand Slam winner, Arthur Ashe, pointed out that many in sport fall victim to, "PARALYSIS BY ANALYSIS". Athletes on any level can experience the pain of overthinking and sabotaging their performance. Blame many traditional methods of teaching and training.

How can we train smarter, not harder? If only our body and mind could perform in a way that's more natural and instinctive. The best athletes have this quality, but many feel it is simply unattainable for them. I assure you IT IS NOT. In this book you will DISCOVER keys in relation to:

Harnessing the superpower of your mind
    Exercises to enhance your feel and senses
    Clutch performing under pressure
    Being a great team member
    Achieving and consistently entering the "Flow" state

PLUS AS A BONUS, you'll also get:

The Perfect Golf Swing In Minutes
    The ways of teaching the golf swing are often lost in translation. They lose effectiveness and do not make use of our NATURAL,

INSTINCTIVE POWERS.

Without expensive and extensive training, you can learn IN JUST MINUTES in the RIGHT WAY whether you are a beginner or highly skilled player.

In this book you will DISCOVER the keys in relation to:

Hitting great shots. TODAY!
  Rising above complex, mechanical thoughts
  Consistently swinging well WITHOUT COUNTLESS TIME spent
  Unique talent you didn't know was ALREADY WITHIN YOU
  Performing beyond what you ever believed possible

Our potential for learning skills at high levels greatly improves, when we understand how to tap into it. Take the first step to gaining the power to adapt, improve, and excel in sports and all areas of life. Read this book.

PERSONAL POWER PLUS FUSION

Real persuasive power comes from focusing on creating context to fit the argument and audience.

"Pissing people off is both inevitable and necessary. This doesn't mean that the goal is pissing people off. Pissing people off doesn't mean you're doing the right things, but doing the right things will almost inevitably piss people off."

- Former U.S. Secretary of State, Colin Powell

Communication and logic skills are a great power. You may think it's only for those with the gift of gab or the highest IQs, but you don't need to be a genius to learn. DISCOVER how to:

Be more persuasive, engaging, and confident in any conversation

Communicate and express yourself assertively with a pinch of panache

Completely transform your personality as desired to become more outgoing, humorous and respected

Find the power of your voice that eluded you in the past for fear or lack of the proper keys to converse and/or argue

PLUS AS A BONUS, you'll also get:

The Self Confidence Evolution for Single Men

Become fluent in the language of self-confidence. It is the most important factor to attract opportunities and successes to get what you want in life.

Use magic of the mind to conquer limiting beliefs

Learn what women really want and the law of attraction

Captivate, engage, and entertain in every interaction with others Play the game of life coolly, calmly, and composed

Take the first step to gaining all the tools needed to be more persuasive, powerful, and creative in all areas of life. Read this book.